# SQUARE

SIENNA LIU

Published by Black Sunflowers Poetry Press
www.blacksunflowerspoetry.com

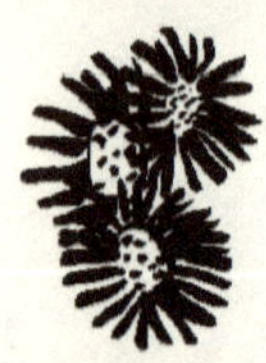



ISBN: 978-1-8382516-9-7

*To L.*

## *Square 1*

I am still living. Recently I've been losing all my pre-conceived notions. I feel little, and belittled. I wondered if there are silences made just for us, just for me. She was talking about pre-school offer seasons in Manhattan, about her two-year-old being told that *This is your escalator to Yale*. I was thinking, why do people make babies. Humans should make a pact to not make babies, ever, so that when we die it's all over. No need for more marauding and hoarding and sinning and rejoicing in sins and repenting and inheriting and remembering and disremembering and being forced to remember. That would be a good short story. When the drinks were finally here I felt reassured, as if the stirring and the shaking and the clinking of the ice against the cold glass could temporarily swallow my own sacrificial ineptitude, with him by my side, a ridiculous twenty-four-year-old reader, looking at me as if I were his prodigal son, and I read in his weighty eyes all the strange sweet sinister words with double meanings. Double weaning. I saw him ageing, gently, shaking the words as I knew them. Chronophobia. Taking an 81% pay cut when you go work for an NGO, that's insane, he said. As long as we don't try that thing called making babies, I said, we will survive.

Harvard Square was the same ingratiated place it always is. We saw a four-year old shouting to hordes of Chinese tourists to get her daily dose of human interaction her parents deny her. We saw college kids with their red Harvard caps and glittering little black dresses. The air was cool and stagnant, the language hallucinated. Someone was singing *Imagine all the people...* sans lyrics. He should list "professional hummer" on his resume. Wholesale imagination, wholesome imagination. Tomorrow we will run faster… I ran. To the store five minutes before closing for the very same "H" cap. Hey, you know what, I'm gonna embroider "-bomb" after the "H". He laughed. It's a sad, sad, sad world we're living in. So I told him. We cast a flinching glance at frozen statues of 200 years of imperialism. Impereaslism. Empirelisme. How do you spell it I don't care. No, you do, you do. He insisted. I'm so afraid. I want to cry my heart out, but what for? Will I be your muse? I'm not an artist. Then you'll be my muse. Yes. You're saying I'm an artist. Yes. Muses wither, muses get bought, muses cease to sing. Look homeward, angel. What? Thomas Wolfe. Of course. Where's home? I wanted to sleep. He was whispering. Let me tell you about my socialist utopia, first... And then, nothing.

*Square 3*

My black bag sailed across the white icy lake. I heard a voice, gathered by the statue of John Harvard, steadily, *Cheese*! A uniform smile. A tailor-made smile. Instructed by a metaphysical prompter. Tempted by the collective unconscious. Commanded by an eternal social need. Herded by a cold lens. They were putting together that smile. A uniform, faceless smile. With the soul behind this mass-produced mask, dried, creased. With the soul non-existent. They were saying *cheese*, again and again, as if they were reminding themselves to smile, as if they were just learning how to smile. I witnessed the smile. I felt like Charles River in early spring. With my feet deep in the snow, I was already melting at the first ray of sun, before I even knew it was the sun. I didn't know how to smile like that. A smile like a wound. *Cheese!* I imagined someone dipping my eyeballs into a fondue pot. Hot and hearty. *Cheese*. I imagined someone stretching the corners of my mouth into a wound. Cheese! What do we have. We have slogans, flags, declarations, and clichés in the present tense. Cheese. Me and my black bag. I wanted to put my head into my black bag and smother myself. So that all reality would disappear, so that I would never know what I was going through.

One snowy day, I was naked in a white room frozen in time. They put many pipes in me, and they deposited me there without telling me why. I could not breathe. The pain above the ribs and below the neck—I deserved it. Many people were protesting, protesting outside the white room, against the ruthlessness of institutions. And I lay there, thinking about him. I would think of anything to avoid thinking about my pain. So I thought about him. I remembered, after seeing him for the first time, I wrote in my diary, 'I was annoyed by his provincialism, and that hierarchy only bothers him when it works against him...' (Kafka wrote, 'World War broke out in the morning, I went swimming in the afternoon.' My history professor said, *I walked past the square that year and saw so many students there, protesting. And I thought, when will they grant my research funding?*) And I thought, if there were no disasters or revolutions, all my non-metaphysical pain would become a joke. Like being forgotten in a white room frozen in time. And I thought, the truly ruthless are the eyes that see people as mere bodies. All the shouts and cries, before and after, all our gestures, futile but grand, were, in the end, nothing but a naked body on the operating table.

### *Square 5*

Never trust people who repeatedly claim to want to turn over a new leaf. I cracked open two fortune cookies. One said to me *you have a heart of gold.* The other said nothing. I looked for it for a long time, but it didn't say a word. In my dream, my little sister walked through a small yard full of weeds, carrying a sugar bun. Grandpa loves those sugar buns, and now I can't find them anymore at the market. In my dream my sister kept walking, and the weeds grew wildly until she disappeared into that endless green stretching towards an end I could not see. No one has gone out for breakfast these days, she told me. But what about food, I asked. Oh there is food, she said, we hoard, and there is a small supermarket still open. Unlike the people who told me, You can't imagine, or, You don't know what it's like if you are not here, she never explained, she didn't complain, as if I would understand it all, as if I should have been familiar with all of this. Do things non-stop, she told me, don't stop. If you stop you will start thinking about them. She said the weather here is very good, with big clouds. She said you should try to live a little lighter.

Farther and farther away from my people, I was having nightmares. I was dreaming of being chased by missiles, of being gang raped and broadcast live, of being tied up and poked at my eyeballs with a pencil, of being ordered to take off my clothes by men in suits and ties with a loudspeaker in Congress. We, all young girls, slowly undressing, glancing at each other, almost with the contempt of revolutionaries, began to mess around with other girls. The men were getting angry while we kissed each other. I was both happy and humiliated. It's always like this. In front of a congress of angry men, even resistance is humiliating. Farther and farther away from my people, I was doing zig-zag puzzles, looking for parts of my people in other people. Some had their voice, some their eyes, and some their smell. I put these pieces together with embarrassment, and then I thought, you can't always live in the past. You can't, always, live in the past. Like a woman searching in the Atacama Desert for the remains of her lover, year after year. I was searching. For the bones of them. For the breaths of them. Others asked me again and again why I want bones. I explained. They never understood. I just want them, I just want those bones too much.

*Square 7*

My mother sent me photos of my sister's wedding. She was crying, crying in each photo. Her makeup ruined, spattered, like an abstract painting. Mother said everyone was crying, it was a weird wedding. I couldn't see her face clearly. The photos were blurred, swollen with her tears. I knew she must be beautiful, but I couldn't see her. She was very still, sedated, and smeared. She was not moving. I thought of the time when she fell asleep on a bus and I touched her fingers, only very slightly, to check if she was still moving. And I thought, my sister she likes to run everywhere, since we were young, everywhere she goes she runs, more quickly than anyone else, and she has been getting big and getting old quickly. Looking at these blurry photos, I feared that she will also die quickly. She is becoming a mother now, in that town. I'm not her, I don't have the right to be empathizing too much. The only thing I can do is to dream more, and watch her walk through that yard one more time, carrying her sugar bun. Now, the yard, ironically, is the yard of an epidemic prevention station, where patients come and go, and she lives in it. A young bride with a young child among the sick and the dying.

For a few days, the city was more apocalyptical than usual, like an old postcard from the future. A marvelous city. A marvelous city that everybody breathing here, even a non-citizen, can claim to be hers. A marvelous failing city that feeds on the idleness of her past, with a stylistic nonchalance that is, at heart, an incompetence. And she knows this all too well, casting a cold eye. Someone in the office was laughing softly. I searched for that laugh, filtered it out from the background noises, squeezed it, and played it over and over again. I wished someone would tell another joke, so that I could hear that laugh again, even though it sounded only slightly, only very slightly, like his laugh. I can't say anything. Better not say it. Otherwise words will become him, replace him. I shouldn't even think, dare not think, dare not think for too long. Life goes on. I put my face on the large window in my office, looking for a portrait of the sea in the shadow. I lied. I couldn't see the sea from my office. But the annoying tu-tu-tu-tu of the helicopter—whose president? Not my president—reminded me that the sea was nearby. Tu-tu-tu-tu. I no longer knew what year this was. Many faces were returning, and each morning was a different era.

She said a lot, and I was surprised that she could keep breathing when she was saying so much. When I mentioned some books and movies, she wasn't interested, but she understood, understood it all, and she almost died trying to understand. She reminded me of my mother. I hadn't seen my mother for three years. Drink, it will be a long day. Did she say it? I was blaming it on her again. Do you like it here? It's very different from what I expected. Nothing is ever as good as I expected. We have the true and the ugly, but they never apologize, no one apologizes. I cannot forgive, I cannot be forgiven. When the subway rushed in, the long-standing myth of the city convinced me that I could jump off the platform and resurrect right there on the spot and climb up the flagpole again. Cards and symbols at the fingertips of Venezuelan poets. Pear-flavored wine. I was soaked in your melancholy syrup, thinking that I was still fresh and clean, like pears just picked from the branches. She started to drink miso soup, like she was drinking water. But I couldn't explain the difference between drinking miso soup and drinking water. We poked the fish with our chopsticks, like an innocuous joke. Why was it so funny, I couldn't explain either.

*Square 10*

I walked in glass. I stepped upon stone. Flying knives were going to pass over my head any minute. Air was being sucked dry. All I could think of, was that there was not enough air for all of us. In front of the glass building, someone acted as if he were praying. He was thin. People who wear pajamas on the street are a disgrace. People who wear guns can swagger through the market. We are alike. On the street we declare our rights, or freedom, or the lack thereof. Now, today, the street is lonely and soft. Large tracts of deserted places, slogans from the 1950s, or barbed wires, visible and invisible. My family was in Xinjiang, my family was in Hubei, and my palms were sweaty. Outside their window was the memorial square, a huge silent object. Why should they be there. Why can I be here. I walked on Wall Street with the shame of a survivor, imagining that they—my family—are still talking and talking, sometimes taking a family portrait with a beauty camera, sometimes making dumplings. The rules were set centuries ago. They are not allowed to write, not allowed to think, not allowed to read, so that they have to talk non-stop, as if once they stop talking and get out of there, it is only death.

*Square 11*

Then he said, do you know the wall in Belfast? Then he said it is fifteen feet tall. Then he said that it is even higher than the Berlin Wall. Then he said that the man who killed twelve people became a mural. Then he said, you think these things are far away from you, but they happened in the very center of Europe (and I thought, but the very center of Europe is very far from me). Then he said, I can no longer turn on the TV nowadays. Then he said, I still remember twenty years ago, I was watching TV, I still remember... Then I couldn't hear him. I cut my sausage rolled up in circles and dipped them into creamy mashed potatoes. Then I thought, hey, I'm eating a bloody thing. I swallowed it. Then we turned to look out our window at the same time. The window became our screen. And we became a portrait for the people passing by. Two plates of half-eaten entrails. He said, love is not looking at one another, but looking in the same direction. Yes, I said. But I thought, what I am seeing, you cannot see. What you are seeing, I cannot see. And there are many more things that neither of us can ever see. I couldn't tell him that, of course.

Halloumi Kebab hanging, dangling. Burnt and crispy, our hearts. And he said (ah how old he looked when he said it), but why, but why, we go down and down and descend into darkness. Now that we become nostalgic about a time almost a decade ago. O meek time. O time of the satiated. Our supreme leaders always smiling like the great Buddha. It's almost like we are trapped in a sequence of toxic relationships and we miss our last great ex who also beat us speechless oh yes they do that too don't they oh yes with a smile too so now we feel really really sad they are not here anymore. We miss a nice beating with a nice smile. (And I let my palm hover over the candlelight.) Anger ruined us, I said. We were fresher back then weren't we? We had proper nostalgia. What is nostalgia, he asked. **Nostalgia**: some mythical sentiment for an uncontaminated past before the process of colonization; and the fabrication of a collective identity to combat the unbearable present. What is proper, he asked. **Proper**: what we consider to be Capital. Then he said, oh but Shanghai but Shanghai. Garlic aioli continued to drip as men continued to speak and garlic is as good as ten mothers and men are as good as they claim to be.

## *Square 13*

How could I ever forget I was in New York? From the terrace on the sixteenth floor, we ended up in a dark karaoke bar. Wine, neat and strong, ate me bit by bit from the stomach, and went upstream. The other girls are all carrying Hermès and Chanel, and I, carrying a Trader Joe's bag, become the coolest person around. I will put this bag on my head the next day, like little animal soldiers in cartoons. We crawled through Chinatown and passed the court, but my head was in a Trader Joe's bag. Deaf, like a metaphor. Let us go back to this terrace again, let us talk, let us say more, and say it better, let us learn to take out our business cards at the right time, learn to squeeze out heart-warming words for compatriots we meet in another country, and let us smile self-consistently. Then we observed more greasy and vulgar sentences jump onto the big screen, then we laughed, ate cake, mouthfuls and mouthfuls of red velvet. Sentences broken, smiles interrupted by clinking glasses, not pretty enough to paste over our walls rich in slogans. We spoke of Beijing, Shanghai, Guangzhou, Shenzhen, glorious peace everywhere, we spoke of the five-year plan, you and me, we are all good, we are all very good, we are all good beyond recognition.

## *Square 14*

Organs in my body, long forgotten by their host, were vying for my attention, as if they were trying to explain, to start a conversation. The other day, I was finally introduced to my stomach. At the time I was having crab cake with truffled cream, petit fours on an elevated plate, and a glass of bubbly. There was also a woman there. She wore an emerald-green three-piece suit, with ridiculously huge eyes, and begged us to ask ourselves this question every morning: are you a brand? (I swallowed my canapé.) The way we do our hair, the way we interact with billionaires, the way we write our briefs or emails or anything, all fall into branding. Be entrepreneurial. (I dug into my crab cake.) She then told the inspirational story of being held at gunpoint, of thinking, *this is not the way my story is gonna end.* (I drank my wine.) That thought was a turning point. She started running. She ran so very beautifully that she was invited to do a documentary running with animals in Tanzania—the representative of homo sapiens in the Great Migration. It was then I had to excuse myself and run to the bathroom to throw up all remnants of the truffled crab cake. The porcelain toilet was watching me, compassionately. I went back to the lunch table.

## *Square 15*

A group of people were dancing by the sidewalk. They seemed happy, functional. I was drawing in large breaths so as not to faint, but I was not running beautifully. I had a copy of 'Difficult Loves' with me, I don't know why. I was not in the mood for Calvino. But I was glad I had it. In the waiting area, the little television was showing women-murdered-by-their-lovers-or-lovers-wanna-be. People watching with enormous interest. Supposedly people who also had mal-functioned organs. Almost an hour later, after the routine check-ups, I was allowed in a second waiting area. Here the little television was showing sensational images of food. I laughed. A guy next to me was reading a Wikipedia entry to his girlfriend, about how doctors first discovered diabetes. *Diabetic urine, the surgeon Herbert Mayo wrote in 1832, is almost always of a pale straw or greenish color. Its smell is commonly faint and peculiar, sometimes resembling sweet whey or milk.* Now a doctor with his five senses approached the guy and discussed his whole medical history in front of me. Guy reading Wikipedia was elated, so elated that he volunteered to contribute to the heroic efforts of the night shift. *So, can I do anything? Unpacking the needles or changing sheets?* The doctor looked at him, compassionately, like he couldn't understand what the guy was saying.

He sat down by me and saw the book I was leafing through. 'Difficult Loves', why? I tried to explain, it's not actually difficult loves, more like difficult lives. Not helpful. We waited. I hate waiting. Waiting in a hospital means prolonged pain, added to professional indifference from all sides. It means being left in a room, naked, cold, surrounded by tubes and beeping machines, not knowing when you are going to be remembered, rediscovered, recognized, re-plugged into some life-sustaining miracle. And we all know miracles don't exist. I told him, I hate hospitals. It has something to do with dignity, or the lack thereof. He said, stop talking like a lawyer. I said, lawyers have feelings too, allegedly. A nurse walked by and patted on my shoulder. Pretty dress, she said. I thanked her and shuddered in my petty prettiness. Someone asked me for my blood, and I gave it. You have anemia, did anyone tell you? No, I never knew. No wonder they never wanted my blood. I have bad blood. He said no, you just have poor blood. A few tubes away, I felt good, for losing some blood. He was looking at me, for the first time in many days. I knew that now, he would finally begin to forgive me. Ah, so, you are this weak? His eyes were saying.

## *Square 17*

He was here with the medicine, and we walked to K-town for ice-cream. We walked very slowly in the sunset, with the lights bouncing back and forth between glass buildings and blinding us momentarily from time to time. I said to him, see, this reminds me of a Chinese poem: I thought that children, must be born by day on purpose. Since you come to this world, you have to look at the sun. With your favorite human— He stopped me there, but you, you are not human. I am not human, I said. Later that day many artists were born, dancing in an old storage room. I hid in their shadows, chewing, thinking, none of this seems unusual. If you write about these things—something something clouds, somebody somebody screams, bridges, horses, villages, knuckles, mothers, a death, a chill—then you are automatically a poet. Everyone can be a poet, everyone who chews. At these events we could always count on food that prevented us from talking to one another. Finger food. Medicine-sized food. We picked them up with our hands. Mini crab cakes potato bites and sausage rolls. My palate was hyper-sensitive to sugar and oil. Burdened, defeated, embarrassed by their lingering gravity. I put half-bitten pieces onto a black napkin and carefully folded it several times and crushed it in my fist.

## *Square 18*

During a supposedly fun icebreaker my colleagues began to talk about where they came from. It was my turn. I said, my family could talk non-stop. They would extend their hands for my face, my body. They touched, weighed, evaluated, talked about why this had happened. On my own soil I was something touchable. On my own soil my mother asked me to "call people." Which is a type of appellation. Why don't you call people? I would say, uncle, grandma, auntie, accompanied with a beaten smile, to people I never met before in my life. On my own soil every fifteen minutes someone would try to force feed me. I explained that I had stomach issues. Then I got tired of explaining, so I just swallowed. On my own soil there are unruly kids, who wear new clothes, turn somersaults, tear up your book, ask for eyeshadow and earrings, sing out-of-tune songs, and everyone else will clap and gasp like they were seeing a miracle. On my own soil whenever I carry my camera outside there will be men with guns following me around. I want to take out my camera to shoot them, but I am too afraid that my teeth tremble. But of course I didn't say any of that. I just said, oh my family, they are very far from here.

## *Square 19*

I was turning twenty-five. He bought me a cake. The cake was saying to me in chocolate: 'this is a cake'. I had to laugh. What shall we do next? I asked. Next, you will have to receive kind blessings, with your ingratiating smile, he said. Next, you will need to light a candle and listen to our old-fashioned song. And next, he said, you have to promise us, all good people with a healthy conscience, that you will continue to live. Year by year. Wow, I said, you have it all planned out. I said, okay, shall I do a toast? He said, let's hear it. And I said, it is thanks to you that I have lived another year. It goes without saying that after three rounds of alcohol everyone is my loyal follower and believer—so I shouldn't be too conceited. Thank you very much for your gift, in any case. Sometimes I want to believe that the gift you bring out is something not easy to come by. You put a very good thing in it. Other times I want to be completely disappointed in you, and be convinced that your heart is truly barren, so that no matter how long and passionate your confession is, I will never, ever, believe it again. He said, good, now let's eat this cake.

## *Square 20*

She said that once, after a meeting, she picked up a suit from the dry cleaner's and rushed to the next meeting. At the foot of this building in southernmost Manhattan, all the men in suits and ties were gathering. Cloudy eyes. Cloudy faces. She ran up the stairs and met hundreds of these eyes. It's like my recurring nightmare, I told her, I'm waiting for the elevator, on the top floor of an abandoned building. The building is empty, and I am shaking because of how empty it is, because I know no place in this world is truly empty. Then, the elevator door opens, and I see a dozen pairs of eyes. They fall on my face like knives. An elevator-full of white men in suits and ties solemnly squeezed together. They look at me. They don't speak. No one comes out. They just look at me. That is the nightmare. She nodded. At the time no one knew what happened. Men pushed her across a bridge. It wasn't the Brooklyn Bridge. They said you shouldn't walk the landmark. The sky was covered with dust and debris. Thousands of people in suits and ties walked humbly in line. Nobody knew where they were going. One person said, we cross the bridge. Everyone was crossing the bridge. No one asked, why? Or, where to?

Speak. I've forgotten how to. At one of the longest dinner tables ever built, I found myself unable to utter a word. The girl next to me, blond, bony, was talking about the Holy Roman Empire as if it were a personal experience. I thought of my dead friend, and the little gap in his chin, and his words like clouds full of rainwater, shameful, for they are full of rainwater. He never knew how pure rainwater can be. At the longest dinner table ever built, I only wanted to talk to him, face to face, with him and no one else. Or to take a walk with him in the dew, with him and no one else. I wanted to ask him, why is it I cannot say goodbye. I have to linger at the door. I have to do one more superfluous gesture, say one more unnecessary sentence. My understanding of goodbye is always longer than what the world can accept. Tell me, how do others manage to leave so quickly? He would never respond. But hey, he probably knew the answer already. He was so smart. For all my questions, he already prepared answers long, long ago. I smiled thinking that. In the white night, I smiled as others laughed. Holy Roman Empire. Ha ha. All the best people are already dead.

When I couldn't see you, I did various things to please you. Beautiful things. And I lingered in front of countless mirrors. You would never see it, but I was still doing these things, as if your eyes were very close. I told you, hey, I did this thing today. You said, great. But our entire existence was under the roof. And our connection was sabotaged by thousands of signal towers. What would be better things? Well, skin, blood vessels, bones, temperature, humid air. I couldn't come up with any words worthy of you. I saw a graveyard I hadn't seen before. I went in, walked, and chatted with them. They were clean, safe. I stood there reading out their names. Names I sometimes wish were mine. Back home, I imagined, everyone was still talking, talking like a thousand wind chimes, about the price of pork, others' divorces, or celebrity gossip, but never the important things. Someone mentioned a forbidden name and was kicked under the dining table. With a book in my hand I sat among bamboo mats, mosquito nets, fans shaking their heads. Grandpa pushed his wheelchair out. He came to me very, very slowly, and he looked at me with a toothless smile. Nerd, he said. That was the only thing he said to me the last few times I saw him.

## *Square 23*

I dreamed about things in the past. I dreamed of millions of people crossing the same bridge, and the bridge collapsed. I went out to see the nearly empty streets. Under the sun, their entire lives spread out on the grass, pots and pans, kids and dog. I wanted to cry my heart out. My guilt for having a roof. My hypocrisy. My useless affections were long and many. He said to me, you might never be happy, but you could never, truly suffer. When he said that we were busy reconstructing memory. We heard a song called 'Yay Chocolate!' back and forth, several times. Marble floor filled with chocolate. Chocolate filling me up from finger to toe. Snakes and Marx. Why wouldn't Anglo-Americans reconstruct their memory? I asked him. I was walking down the street, hoping that someone would rush towards me this moment and knock me down. I heard that many people who looked just like me had been knocked down, beaten up, killed. I was a walking statement, simply by being alive. Take this breath out of me this minute and I wouldn't really mind. I wouldn't take it too personally. After all, everything is already limp. Pain is limp. Politics is limp. Transaction is limp. Soggy. Drunk. Sunless. Moral judgment, immoral judgment. In the end, everyone has their own private ambitions.

You asked me when I would return to China. I said I don't know. You recited an old Chinese poem: 'You asked me when I shall return, that I have no idea.' You missed the age when people spoke poetry. In Ancient China you said, I would meet you on the street by accident, and I would be so happy to see you that I gave you a poem on the spot. Some inopportune rain had just descended and together we saw with our rose-colored glasses a time that never belonged to us, a place where we only had second-hand memories. With lakes like cool mirrors and moon falling into our porcelain wine cups, we greeted, chanted, we moved our limbs and bodies. While days got wet we drank our hearts numb and stood wistfully at the borders of farewell. A conversation or silence that never ended. One of us was banished or demoted to a terrible province, while the other was never recognized, or not recognized for the right reasons, before our hair began to snow. We looked at one another and spoke of peach flowers and cold water and swan geese in the clouds and the marks from your horse's hoofs in the snow and new grass of next year. Yes, poems like that we used to know. And now. The bridge collapsed.

## *Square 25*

I pick up my pen and shrink like a raisin. The people I love already surpassed their imageries. What are better things? I want to see you again. Tap once on the telephone. We are hibernating, wrapped up in poppies and memories, waiting for the next glorious morning, fresh as the first morning on earth. Day after day. Day after day we look down at our bodies, without shame or apology, bodies in clean little squares, bodies painted and dreamed, bodies fictionalized. The belated tears of my mother, locked up in her Shanghai apartment for thirty-seven days. She texted me to say, 'I crave freedom'. I look at the sky and think ah, 'when shall we be able to trim wicks again, by your Western Window.' The pigeon on my balcony has a swollen foot and each city is pretending to be Shanghai: London, Amsterdam, Paris, Palma. Cold European cities with no patience for my pen. Another spring comes and people die more thoroughly. People get famous quickly and throw themselves off balconies with potted gardenias en plein air. Tap once on the telephone. Little things. Like walking in the sun, stopping near a sycamore tree. To see you again, face to face, and you will count the time they confiscated so that you are now many years behind. Ah all those years, you say.

## Acknowledgements

A longer version of Square 12 appeared in *A Velvet Giant*, Issue 8, 2022.

To Amanda and Black Sunflowers Poetry Press: Thank you. This book is possible because of you.

Friends and family in Shanghai, Tokyo, Boston and New York, I think of you.

**Black Sunflowers Poetry Press**

Backed by an array of artists, activists, poets and poetry fans from all walks of life, Black Sunflowers, the UK's first crowdfunded poetry press, came into being in March 2020 with a pledge to publish and promote the work of women, older women and Black poets from the UK and around the world.

www.blacksunflowerspoetry.com

www.ingramcontent.com/pod-product-compliance
Lightning Source LLC
Chambersburg PA
CBHW021254200726
48288CB00016B/3185

* 9 7 8 1 8 3 8 2 5 1 6 9 7 *